W9-BGM-530

friend

These quotations were gathered lovingly but unscientifically over several years and/or contributed by many friends or acquaintances. Some arrived, and survived in our files, on scraps of paper and may therefore be imperfectly worded or attributed. To the authors, contributors and original sources, our thanks, and where appropriate, our apologies.—The Editors

CREDITS

Compiled by Kobi Yamada
Designed by Steve Potter

ISBN: 978-1-888387-62-9

©2007 Compendium, Incorporated. All rights reserved. No part of this publication may be reproduced or transmitted in any form or by any means, electronic or mechanical, including photocopy, recording, or any storage and retrieval system now known or to be invented without written permission from the publisher. Contact: Compendium, Inc., 600 North 36th St., Suite 400, Seattle, WA 98103. Friend, The Good Life, Celebrating the Joy of Living Fully, Compendium, live inspired and the format, design, layout and coloring used in this book are trademarks and/or trade dress of Compendium Incorporated. This book may be ordered directly from the publisher, but please try your local bookstore first. Call us at 800-91-IDEAS or come see our full line of inspiring products at www.live-inspired.com.
4th Printing. 5K 06 07

Printed in China

Friend. Good.

FRANKENSTEIN'S MONSTER

Life is about sharing.

YOKO ONO

While the right friends are near us, we feel that all is well. Our every-day life blossoms suddenly into bright possibilities.

HELEN KELLER

When I choose a friend—I choose one who loves truth, who respects life and me, one who hears music and sees the moon, one who loves to see me smiling.

LAURA MERZ

Nobody,

but nobody,

can make it

out here

alone.

MAYA ANGELOU

No matter what

accomplishments

you make in life,

somebody

helps you.

WILMA RUDOLPH

THOSE WHOM WE SUPPORT HOLD US UP IN LIFE.

MARIE VON EBNER-ESCHENBACH

WHEREVER WE ARE, IT IS OUR FRIENDS
THAT MAKE OUR WORLD.

HENRY DRUMMOND

When we seek
for connection,
we restore the
world to
wholeness.
Our seemingly
separate lives
become
meaningful
as we discover
how truly
necessary we
are to each
other.

MARGARET WHEATLEY

I THINK WE'RE HERE FOR EACH OTHER.

CAROL BURNETT

the good life™

Celebrating the joy of living fully.

Also available are these spirited
companion books in The Good Life
series of great quotations:

drive
heart
hero
joy
moxie
refresh
service
spirit
success
thanks
value
vision
welcome
yes!

IN THE END, WHAT

AFFECTS YOUR LIFE

MOST DEEPLY ARE

THINGS TOO SIMPLE

TO TALK ABOUT.

NELL BLAINE

With each
true friendship,
we build more firmly
the foundation
on which
the peace of
the whole world
rests.

MAHATMA GANDHI

Treasure each other

in the recognition that

we do not know

how long we shall

have each other.

JOSHUA LOTH LIEBMAN

Never shall I forget the time I spent with you. Please continue to be my friend and you will always find me yours.

LUDWIG VON BEETHOVEN

Thanks for
showing me that
even on the darkest,
rainiest days the sun
is still there,
just behind the clouds,
waiting to shine again.

LISA HARLOW

MY LIFETIME LISTENS TO YOURS.

MARGARET PETERS

Friends are
those rare
people who
ask how
we are, and
then wait
to hear the
answer.

ED CUNNINGHAM

She's the kind of person

who'd go through hell,

high water, or a

paper shredder

for a pal.

KATHI MAIO

WHAT ONE CANNOT, ANOTHER CAN.

SIR WILLIAM DAVENANT

People say
I've had a hard life,
but I've also had
very good company
along the way.

HELEN KELLER

I wish you
sunshine on your
path and storms to
season your journey.
I wish you peace
in the world in which
you live and in the
smallest corner
of the heart where
truth is kept...
More I cannot
wish you except
perhaps love to
make all the rest
worthwhile.

ROBERT A. WARD

REMINDING ONE ANOTHER

OF THE DREAM THAT EACH

OF US ASPIRES TO MAY

BE ENOUGH FOR US TO

SET EACH OTHER FREE.

ANTOINE DE SAINT-EXUPÉRY

I ONLY WISH
YOU COULD SEE
WHAT I SEE
WHEN I
LOOK AT YOU.

KOBI YAMADA

A FRIEND IS SOMEONE WHO
MAKES IT EASY TO BELIEVE IN YOURSELF.

HEIDI WILLS

Anything,
everything,
little or big,
becomes
an adventure
when the
right person
shares it.

KATHLEEN NORRIS

Friendship?

Yes, please.

CHARLES DICKENS

DO YOU KNOW
THE WONDER OF
WALKING INTO A ROOM
AND HAVING PEOPLE HAPPY
BECAUSE YOU ARE THERE?
THAT'S THE GREATEST THING.

LEO BUSCAGLIA

FRIENDSHIP BLOSSOMS
WHEN TWO PEOPLE SAY
TO EACH OTHER,
IN EFFECT: "WHAT? YOU TOO?
I THOUGHT I WAS
THE ONLY ONE!"

C.S. LEWIS

It seems to me that trying to live without friends is like milking a bear to get cream for your morning coffee. It's a whole lot of trouble, and then not worth much after you get it.

ZORA   NEALE   HURSTON

A friend is someone who
will bail you out of jail.
A best friend is the one sitting
next to you saying,
"Boy that was fun."

JACK MILLER

My friend is not perfect,

no more than I, and so we

suit each other admirably.

ALEXANDER POPE

WE'VE BEEN THROUGH
SO MUCH
TOGETHER—AND
MOST OF IT
WAS YOUR FAULT.

LAUREN ROTHCHILD

Thanks for teaching me right

from wrong...I especially

liked the "wrong" part.

M.D. O'CONNER

True humor
is fun—it does
not put down, kid,
or mock.
It makes people
feel wonderful,
not separate, different,
and cut off.
True humor has
beneath it
the understanding
that we are all
in this together.

HUGH PRATHER

THAT IS THE BEST—
TO LAUGH WITH SOMEONE BECAUSE
YOU BOTH THINK THE SAME
THINGS ARE FUNNY.

GLORIA VANDERBILT

Laughter is
not at all a bad
beginning
for a friendship,
and it is by far
the best ending
for one.

OSCAR WILDE

Shared laughter creates a bond of friendship. When people laugh together, they cease to be young and old, teacher and pupils, worker and boss. They become a single group of human beings.

W. LEE GRANT

Real friends are those who,

when you've made a fool of yourself,

don't feel that you've done

a permanent job.

ERWIN T. RANDALL

I am so glad you are here.
It helps me to realize how
beautiful my world is.

RAINER MARIA RILKE

WINTER,

SPRING, SUMMER

OR FALL…ALL YOU'VE

GOT TO DO IS CALL…AND I'LL BE THERE,

YES I WILL…YOU'VE GOT A FRIEND.

CAROLE KING

Old memories

are so empty when

they cannot be

shared.

JEWELLE GOMEZ

I always knew I would

look back at the times

I'd cried, and laugh.

But I never knew that I'd

look back at the times

I'd laughed and cry.

SHAUN PROWDZIK

Time has
a wonderful
way of
showing us
what really
matters.

MARGARET PETERS

When being together

is more important

than what you do,

you are with a friend.

CONNIE McMARTIN

LIFE IS TO BE FORTIFIED

BY MANY FRIENDSHIPS.

TO LOVE AND BE LOVED

IS THE GREATEST

HAPPINESS OF EXISTENCE.

SYDNEY SMITH

Throughout life, one does not miss any chance to hold onto the things that are really precious, if one is truly wise.

ED GREENWOOD

Love and
kindness are
never wasted.
They always
make a
difference.

HELEN JAMES

FAMILIAR ACTS ARE BEAUTIFUL THROUGH LOVE.

PERCY BYSSHE SHELLEY

It's the
little things we
do and say
that mean
so much
as we go
our way.

WILLA HOEY

THROUGH LOVE, THROUGH FRIENDSHIP,
A HEART LIVES MORE THAN ONE LIFE.

ANAÏS NIN

We have a great deal more friendship than is ever spoken. How many persons we meet in houses, whom yet we honor, and who will honor us! How many we see in the street, or sit with in church, whom, though silently, we warmly rejoice to be with. Read the language of these wandering eye-beams. The heart knoweth.

RALPH WALDO EMERSON

THE UNIVERSE IS MADE OF STORIES, NOT OF ATOMS.

MURIEL RUDEYSER

Relationships create the fabric of our lives. They are the fibers that weave all things together.

EDEN FROUST

When

friends ask,

there is no

tomorrow…

only now.

ALEXANDER DREY

I felt it shelter to speak to you.

EMILY DICKINSON

We all need something to believe in, something for which we can have whole-hearted enthusiasm. We need to feel that our life has meaning, that we are needed in this world.

HANNAH SENESH

What greater thing is there

for two human souls than

to feel that they are

joined...to strengthen

each other...to be one

with each other in silent

unspeakable memories.

GEORGE ELIOT